DEBORAH SAMPSON

by Laura K. Murray

PEBBLE
a capstone imprint

Pebble Explore is published by Pebble, an imprint of Capstone.
1710 Roe Crest Drive
North Mankato, Minnesota 56003
www.capstonepub.com

Library of Congress Cataloging-in-Publication Data
Names: Murray, Laura K., author.
Title: Deborah Sampson / Laura K. Murray.
Description: North Mankato, Minnesota : Pebble, an imprint of Capstone, [2021] | Series: Biographies | Includes bibliographical references and index. | Audience: Ages 6–8 | Audience: Grades 2–3 | Summary: "How much do you know about Deborah Sampson? Find out the facts you need to know about this woman who fought in the Revolutionary War. You'll learn about the early life, challenges, and major accomplishments of this important American"—Provided by publisher.
Identifiers: LCCN 2020030652 (print) | LCCN 2020030653 (ebook) | ISBN 9781977132062 (hardcover) | ISBN 9781977133083 (paperback) | ISBN 9781977154088 (ebook)
Subjects: LCSH: Gannett, Deborah Sampson, 1760–1827—Juvenile literature. | United States—History—Revolution, 1775–1783—Participation, Female—Juvenile literature. | Women soldiers—United States—Biography—Juvenile literature. | Soldiers—United States—Biography—Juvenile literature.
Classification: LCC E276.G36 M87 2021 (print) | LCC E276.G36 (ebook) | DDC 973.3092 [B]—dc23
LC record available at https://lccn.loc.gov/2020030652
LC ebook record available at https://lccn.loc.gov/2020030653

Image Credits
Alamy: Science History Images, cover, 1, 27; Bridgeman Images: © Look and Learn, 15, Gift in memory of Beatrice Weeks Bostock, 19; Getty Images: De Agostini Picture Library, 18, Kean Collection, 13; Granger: 7, 16, 20, 22; Library of Congress: 21; Line of Battle Enterprise: 11; North Wind Picture Archives: 5, 8, 10, 12, 29, Nancy Carter, 25; Shutterstock: Curly Pat (geometric background), cover, back cover, 2, 29; U.S. Navy: Photo by Mass Communication Specialist 3rd Class Neo B. Greene III, 26

Editorial Credits
Editor: Erika L. Shores; Designer: Elyse White; Media Researcher: Svetlana Zhurkin; Production Specialist: Spencer Rosio

Table of Contents

Words in **bold** are in the glossary.

Who Was Deborah Sampson?

Deborah Sampson was an American soldier. She was one of the first women to serve in the U.S. **military**. She fought in the **Revolutionary War** (1775–1783). After this war, the United States was its own country.

Deborah dressed as a man so she could fight. At that time, women were not allowed to be soldiers. Deborah joined the army in **disguise**. She worked as a **scout**. She fought bravely. Today, there are still many questions about her life.

Growing Up Deborah

Deborah was born December 17, 1760 in Plympton, Massachusetts. Massachusetts was one of the 13 British **colonies**. It was ruled by Great Britain.

Deborah had six brothers and sisters. Her family did not have much money. They were poor farmers. When Deborah was five, her father left the family. Deborah's mother did not have enough money to take care of the children. She sent them to live with other people.

In the 1700s, children often did farmwork alongside their parents.

Colonial girls helped with household chores such as making butter.

When Deborah was 10, she moved in with a new family. She worked for them but did not get paid. They gave her food and shelter. They didn't let her go to school because she was a girl. But they taught her at home.

Deborah learned all she could. She learned how to sew, hunt, ride horses, and farm. She was good at making things. She made tools and items from wood.

Joining the Army

At age 18, Deborah was free to live on her own. She took jobs as a teacher. She made money from weaving. But Deborah wanted to do something new. She looked for adventure.

a teacher with her students in a colonial one-room school

American soldiers battled the British in 1777.

The Revolutionary War had begun a few years earlier. Colonists felt that Great Britain ruled them unfairly. Many colonists joined together to fight the British. Deborah wanted to fight too. But women were not allowed.

Men could join the colonial army at recruiting offices.

When Deborah was 21, she had an idea. She would pretend to be a man so she could fight. In early 1782, Deborah joined the army in Middleborough, Massachusetts. She tied her hair back. She put on boys' clothing. But she was quickly found out.

In May 1782, Deborah tried again. She went to a different town in Massachusetts and joined the army. She used the name Robert Shurtleff. This time, her secret stayed safe for a long time.

Deborah joined the army on her second try.

Fighting for America

Deborah served in the army for 17 months. She was part of the Light Infantry Troops. They served in New York's Hudson Valley. These troops had to be strong and fast. They carried few supplies. They took part in dangerous **raids** and fights.

In June 1782, Deborah and two other leaders took 30 soldiers on a scouting mission. They fought the enemy. Another time, Deborah led a raid that captured 15 men.

Women helped American soldiers who were hurt in battle.

Deborah was hurt several times. But she kept fighting. She was cut by a sword. She was shot in the shoulder and the leg. She dug part of a **musket** ball out of her leg herself. She did not want doctors to find out her secret.

In summer 1783, Deborah's group was sent to Philadelphia. She became sick with fever. A doctor found out she was a woman. But he did not turn her in. His family took care of her.

After the War

The war ended in September 1783. America had won. It was free to be its own country. When Deborah was healed, the doctor told the army her secret. She did not get in trouble. In October 1783, Deborah was **honorably discharged** in West Point, New York. She was 22 years old.

Leaders met in Paris, France, in 1783 to end the war.

a dress worn by Deborah after she left the army

After the war, Deborah met Benjamin Gannett, a farmer from Massachusetts. They married on April 7, 1785. They had three children named Earl, Mary, and Patience. Then they adopted a daughter named Susannah.

Male soldiers were paid for their war service. But Deborah was not, because she was a woman. For years, Deborah asked the **government** to be paid. In 1792, she finally received the pay.

Soldiers returned home after the war. They were paid for their service.

DEBORAH SAMPSON.
Published by H. Mann. 1797.

A book about Deborah's adventures during the war was published in 1797.

Five years later, Deborah met writer Herman Mann. He wrote a book about Deborah's time during the war. The stories were exciting, but they were not all true.

In 1802, Deborah traveled around the country. She gave speeches about being in the army. She was one of the first women in U.S. history to earn money speaking.

United States ――

Massachusetts District ――

Deborah Gannett, of Sharon, in the county of Norfolk, and district of Massachusetts, a resident and native of the United States, and applicant for a pension from the United States, under an Act of Congress entitled an Act to provide for certain persons engaged in the land and naval service of the United States, in the revolutionary war, maketh oath, That she served as a private soldier, under the name of Robert Shurtleff, in the army of the revolution, upwards of two years in manner following viz ―― Enlisted in April 1781. in the company commanded by Captain George Webb ―― in the Massachusetts Regiment commanded then by Colonel Shepherd ―― and afterwards by Colonel Henry Jackson ―― and served in said corps, in Massachusetts and New York ―― until November 1783 ―― when she was honorably discharged in writing, which discharge is lost ―― During the time of her service, she was at the capture of Lord Cornwallis ―― was wounded at Tarrytown ―― and now receives a pension from the United States, which pension she hereby relinquishes ―― She is in such reduced circumstances, as to require the aid of her country ―― for her support ――

                                        Deborah Gannett

Mass. Dist. Sept. 14. 1818

Sworn to before me

M D Davis
Dis Judge
Mass. Dist.

Deborah wrote this letter to prove that she earned a pension.

Deborah kept working to be paid fairly. Male soldiers were paid a **pension** after the war. But Deborah was not given one because she was a woman. Her friend Paul Revere tried to help. He wrote to the government. In 1805, Deborah became the only woman from the war to get a full pension.

Years later, Deborah became sick with yellow fever. On April 29, 1827, Deborah died in Sharon, Massachusetts. She was 66 years old. After she died, government leaders called her a hero.

Remembering Deborah

Today, people keep learning about Deborah's life. They remember her bravery. In 1983, Massachusetts named Deborah the state heroine. May 23 is Deborah Sampson Day in the state. People dress up like Deborah and tell stories about her life.

Deborah is remembered in other ways too. There is a sign in her hometown of Plympton, Massachusetts. In the town of Sharon, people can visit a house and a park named for her.

a statue of Deborah outside the Sharon Public Library

Deborah was not the only woman to fight in the Revolutionary War. But she is one of the best known. She showed that women can be skilled soldiers. She spoke out for fair pay. Today, many women serve in the U.S. military.

Women serve in all U.S. military branches, including the U.S. Navy.

Deborah presents a letter describing her brave service in the army.

Deborah Sampson was a daring hero of American history. People said a woman could not fight. But Deborah knew they were wrong. She wanted to serve her country. Her strength and bravery helped America win the war.

Important Dates

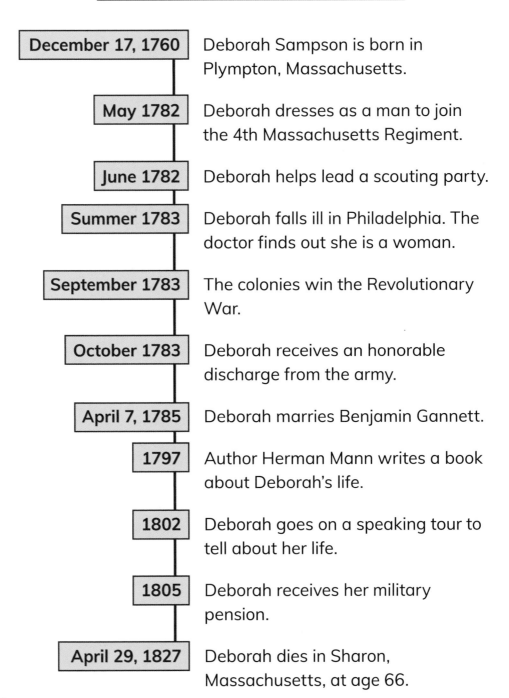

December 17, 1760	Deborah Sampson is born in Plympton, Massachusetts.
May 1782	Deborah dresses as a man to join the 4th Massachusetts Regiment.
June 1782	Deborah helps lead a scouting party.
Summer 1783	Deborah falls ill in Philadelphia. The doctor finds out she is a woman.
September 1783	The colonies win the Revolutionary War.
October 1783	Deborah receives an honorable discharge from the army.
April 7, 1785	Deborah marries Benjamin Gannett.
1797	Author Herman Mann writes a book about Deborah's life.
1802	Deborah goes on a speaking tour to tell about her life.
1805	Deborah receives her military pension.
April 29, 1827	Deborah dies in Sharon, Massachusetts, at age 66.

Fast Facts

Name:
Deborah Sampson

Role:
soldier in Revolutionary War

Life dates:
December 17, 1760 to April 29, 1827

Key accomplishments:
Deborah Sampson dressed as a man so she could fight in the Revolutionary War. She kept her secret even when she was hurt. She fought to receive the same pay as male soldiers.

Glossary

colony (KAH-luh-nee)—an area that has been settled by people from another country and is owned by that country

disguise (dis-GYZ)—something that hides what a person really looks like

government (GUHV-urn-muhnt)—the group of people who make rules and decisions for a country or state

honorably discharged (ON-uhr-blee DIS-charj-duh)—when someone is allowed to leave the military after serving with honor

military (MIL-uh-ter-ee)—the armed forces of a country

musket (MUHSS-kit)—a gun carried on the shoulder

pension (PEN-shuhn)—a regular payment a person gets after they retire

raid (RAYD)—a surprise attack

Revolutionary War (rev-uh-LOO-shuhn-air-ee WOR)—the American colonies' fight from 1775 to 1783 for freedom from Great Britain

scout (SKOWT)—a soldier that is sent ahead to find out information

Read More

Loh-Hagan, Virginia. *Girl Warriors*. Ann Arbor, MI: Cherry Lake Publishing, 2020.

Marsh, Sarah Glenn. *Anna Strong: A Daughter of the American Revolution*. New York: Abrams Books for Young Readers, 2020.

Marsico, Katie. *Sybil Ludington's Revolutionary War Story*. Minneapolis: Lerner, 2018.

Internet Sites

Deborah Sampson: Brooklyn Museum
www.brooklynmuseum.org/eascfa/dinner_party/heritage_floor/deborah_sampson

Deborah Sampson: National Women's History Museum
www.womenshistory.org/education-resources/biographies/deborah-sampson

Legends of America: Deborah Sampson Gannett—Lady Soldier in the American Revolution
www.legendsofamerica.com/deborah-sampson-gannett/

Index